You Matter Most! Advice
Season One: Attraction, Intimacy, & Sex

Dr. Ethan Gregory

First Edition

DEDICATION

Special thanks to Veronica Cannon and Katie Pegler. In 2006, I was searching for gigs on Craigslist, looking to start making my mark in the self-help industry. I was lucky enough to find someone looking for writers for 944 Magazine. I was on Myspace, giving advice there, and was helping people with their relationship issues. I began writing a column for the online content at 944 Orange County, and that began a weekly column I called the *944 911*.

Two years later I moved overseas and stopped the column. While 944 is no longer with us, the editors allowed me to spread my wings and practice putting the Ethan Gregory Approach into words. *The 911* is back online now, at www.drethangregory.com with an even more diverse range of topics to learn from.

CONTENTS

INTRODUCTION TO THE EGA

The core of the Ethan Gregory Approach is that we need to make sure we are healthy, and must ensure our own emotional security to best interact with others in our lives. If we are not being safe with our lifestyle, we can't enhance the lives of others. I am often told that I am a giver, and I do go out of my way to help anyone that I can. For the most part, that is true. However, I could not do that if I was not ensuring my own health and protecting myself within my relationships.

The other side of that coin is that I am quick to say "No thank you" when I feel something is not in my best interest, or in the best interest of another person. Through the pages of this book you will read advice on a range of very personal issues. Within each response you will see how I advocate the solution that benefits the advice asker, and does the least amount of harm to the other party. Take the lessons within the advice to heart. You can be unselfish and sacrifice many things, but we have to take care of ourselves along the way to keep balance in our life. That, my friend, is why you matter most! I have separated the topics into chapters for you to scroll through. Live through the lives of the question askers, and empathize along with me as I share how to use the EGA to solve their issue. You may not agree with my perspective, and that is fine. If you have a different perspective, feel free to offer your insights to me at the You Matter Most! website. I would love to hear how you utilize the EGA as well. In my previous books, dating manuals allow the reader to practice the EGA through the courtship process. If you have not read through one of them, you can see exactly how the EGA works in the real world. Check out the *I'm Sorry* series after you finish *Season One*.

SEXUALITY
Mr. Funny Feeling

"My girlfriend has a close male friend that she hangs out with all the time. She tells me he is gay, but I can't help but to get jealous sometimes, because she seems to be having a good time with him. As the boyfriend, I don't want to come off as possessive or crazy, but I feel like I am being left out, and I am not sure that he really is gay. What can I do?"

Your gut is telling you all you need to know about this situation. As "the boyfriend" you are entitled to meet the friends of your partner. Tell her you are setting up a dinner party for the upcoming weekend. Your girlfriend would most likely not hesitate to interject herself into a relationship you had with any woman, so why should you? The setup begins when you ask your girlfriend for this guy's phone number. Tell her you want to invite him personally. If she hesitates, something might be up. Invite your gay friend for an extra gaydar (you know you have one). The trap is set.

See where his attention goes. Talk with him about his coming out story, and some details of his last relationship. If the answers aren't flowing off his tongue, or your girl is finishing his story for him, be suspicious. If this guy pays more attention to your girl then he does anything else, there might be a problem. If after that night your girl stops hanging out with him or you, you have your answer. I may be coming off as paranoid, but I have been on the other end of that exchange.

Once I was staying at the Hard Rock in Chicago and met a girl at the bar. As we were going to bed, she asks me if I have ever hooked up with a dude. She tells me that she thinks I am gay, and it is ok because she will still hook up with me even though she is engaged. I didn't do anything to change her mind. She made me out to be something so she could have less guilt about her naughty behavior. You might be her fiancé. Think about that. Best of luck, remember, you matter most!

Mrs. Senator Craig

"I have been dating my boyfriend for three months. My feelings are beginning to get deep for him, but I found out something about his past that has me worried. Before meeting me, he was in a relationship with a man. He passed it off as a brief fling, but I later found out that it was a year long relationship. I am not going to be a woman that marries a man and then finds out he is having an affair with a man, and I am sort of worried about my risk for STD's. Should I stay with this man since he says that he is not gay and he wants to live a Christian life?"

In most relationships there is that awkward conversation about past lovers and relationships, but your situation goes beyond that. The man that you are dating must be pretty open minded to have success with both sexes, but why a Christian life? Your concerns are certainly valid, and I believe they are universal with all people in relationships.

First, let me ease your mind about the stereotypical scary stuff like STD's. The quickest way to tell if you or he has more than meets the eye is to get a test together. Since you are just now taking the condom off it is an appropriate time to have a date getting tested. He will probably appreciate your concern for his and your own safety. Old school blood tests can take up to three weeks to get results, but there are now cheek swabs that can return almost instant results.

Just as important to your physical health is your emotional well-being. Whether your boyfriend is straight or bisexual, you deserve to have the faith in his character that he will not stray from your relationship at any time, unless he officially ends it before he does (or right after, things do happen).

You need to know that your partner is 100% committed to being with you and not to any other person be they gay or straight. The best indicator of future behavior is past behavior, so I have extreme (very extreme) doubts that your boyfriend can go the rest of his life without acknowledging his emotional and physical desires to be with another man. Some experts believe that we are all on a continuum of sexuality, and your boyfriend may be somewhere in the middle as far as his attractions goes. You may have more security in your life if you have a man that is interested in women only, but you are still at risk for him cheating, like in any relationship.

What you need to determine is why your boyfriend is making the switch. If he needs to pray each night that he doesn't wake up gay, then you are in trouble. Have the conversation with him about why he entered into his same sex relationship, and why he entered your relationship. If he uses religion as motivation, or he comes across as minimizing his emotional attachment to his last relationship while pledging his love to you, you have to be wary. If it doesn't feel right to you, then you won't be comfortable in the relationship long term, so better to end it now and move on to someone that will make you feel more secure. But, it doesn't mean that you can't stay in this person's life. Beware of anyone that feels an active need to cover up or deny parts of his or her life. Best of luck, remember that you matter most!

Mr. If You See Them Point Them Out

"I have a new friend that I think might be gay. He is a super friendly person that seems to be ambiguous when it comes to attraction to both guys and girls. None of the people I know have ever seen him hitting on either women or men. I am thinking about asking him if he swings either way. He has a tattoo on the small of his back, but his voice and mannerisms are not flamboyant or feminine. Is it wrong to ask someone about their sexuality if they don't advertise it?"

Society is big on labels. We want to know if someone is wearing *Gucci* or *No Boundaries*, and we want to know where everyone stands when it comes to their sexuality. People always ask each other about possible visiting team players because of the general assumption that we all play for the home team. When we find people that go against our expectations and live outside of our comfort zones, we want to think that they are somehow different from us. In fact, they are not. We all need to understand that whom we do does not put us on separate teams; it just means we play different positions.

Before you yank your friend out of the closet, you should think about why you want to know. Are you gay and attracted to him? If not, it

8

might be for the sake of putting a label on the unknown, and that isn't a great reason to do something. What does knowing whether he plays pitcher or catcher do for you? If your friend thought you should know about who he wants to fall in love with, he would tell you.

Until he does, try to be comfortable with his ambiguity until he decides he is comfortable with sharing his sexuality with you. I don't see the harm in asking, but be prepared for any answer. I would ask if he has a sexual preference or if he thinks about being gay, not a direct question about sexuality. He is leaving out details for a reason, and you need to respect that. You were his friend before you knew, and you had better be his friend after he tells you. Best of luck, and remember that you matter most!

Mr. Bi-Curious

"I have a friend that I have known for over 10 years. We are both single males and we are very comfortable around each other. I have never considered myself to be attracted to him in a homosexual way, but I am beginning to wonder about my sexuality. I have been with women only, but I have always wanted to see what it was like with a man. I am thinking about letting my friend know, and asking him if I could kiss him to see how it feels, since I am almost positive that he won't hold it against me. What do you think?"

Good for you taking time to decide where you are on that continuum of sexuality. Just because you are not John Wayne, doesn't mean you are Richard Simmons. For some people it takes time after those peer-pressured high school and college years to settle into a sexuality preference. There is nothing wrong with doing some research.

About your friend, I wouldn't pucker up to him just yet. You might want to throw out some debate on the idea of homosexuality if you haven't already. See where he stands on the issue, and then ask him directly how he would feel about you if you were gay. Even if he says that he will be your wingman at the local gay club, I don't think a make out session between old friends is the best way to gauge your interest in strange men.

I think it is safe to say that close male friends are already man-crushing on their buddies enough to have emotional connections that run deep. I know that I love my close male friends, but if I was to experiment with my sexuality they would not be lining up for batting practice (well, some of them might). My advice is to take your research into the club, where you can test your urges on anonymous people with whom you have no attachments. That way, feelings of emotional and physical are not blended. If your friend is truly a good friend and not an ignorant bigot, they will accept your curiosity and won't judge you in a negative way.

Like any new experience, make sure that you don't confuse apprehension and fear with lack of desire. Throw yourself into the fire on your terms, and decide if you want to jump out or warm up to the idea of a new you. Best of luck, remember that you matter most!

Mr. Red Pill or Blue Pill

"I was raised with a Christian background. My family is deeply religious. I have always thought that I was attracted to men, but I have never tried to act on my feelings. I have a lot of guilt and confusion about how I want to live. I have not dated before, guy or girl. What should I do about these weird feelings?"

You seem to be at a crossroads about how you want your life to go. There is no real societal advantage to living a gay lifestyle, especially when you know that your family and friends are going to tell you that you are about to burn in hell for all eternity, or whatever it says in the bible. The feelings you are having might be part of puberty, depending on your age, but there is only one way to find out if one gender fits better as a partner, and that is to try both on. If you are already getting the tingles for dudes, then you are, at a minimum, open to the idea of some man on man love.

There is nothing at all wrong with that, but obviously you are going to have to get away from the parents and close circle of friends to test the waters. What I recommend is that you go to the closest age-appropriate LGBT meet up, and talk to some people there. Get their stories and see if you feel comfortable. If you feel like the people there are your people, then by all means jump from grey to gay.

I would follow up your night out with one that places you in contact with someone that is desirable. Start watching porn to see where your interests are. Focus on embracing your needs while coming to terms with the potential reactions of close friends and family. If they choose to lose you, then they are the losers.

What I want you to think hard about is resisting the down low lifestyle. Part of growing up is defining who you are and what you want to be. If you are emotionally attracted to men, but you choose the straight life, you will end up a 50-something man reaching under a toilet stall in an airport bathroom. Spare yourself and your fake wife the shame. You can still have everything you would want in life if you are openly homosexual, the only differences will be that you will have sex with mangina instead of vagina, and you will be truly happy.

If you live in an isolated area and fear being killed, then it is time to start looking at colleges in the big city. Finding out what feels good doesn't work if you are the victim of a hate crime. Be smart, be brave, be yourself. Best of luck, remember that you matter most!

Mr. Cleaning Out the Closet

"What makes someone gay? My friend of five years just told me that he was gay. I have seen him hook up with girls, he has even had relationships with women. I don't really care that he likes guys, but why the big change all of a sudden? With the way that gay people are treated in our society it doesn't seem like a wise choice. "

Your question is still a debated topic among people in the behavior business. There is one school of thought that believes that sexual preference is something that is set in stone from birth. A person is born gay or straight. Another perspective is that sexual identity is developed over the life span, through ones experiences and upbringing. The term used by the researchers for the debate is nature vs. nurture. What I believe, is that people are born somewhere along the spectrum from *The Birdcage* to *Conan the Barbarian*. How they choose to live their life will dictate the way that their sexuality is expressed or repressed.

Your friend seems to be a good example of repression turning into expression. Most guys grow up learning that gay is something wrong or bad to be. We call each other gay when we mean effeminate or weak. There is no place for expression during ones youth. Usually when we get to college, whether you are gay or straight, is when we start to come into our own sexual identities. We are free from old stereotypes about ourselves, and our parents are not around.

Depending on ones upbringing, some people never act on their sexual preference. You hear a story of men in their 40's having gay relationships while they are married and have children. If you were brought up to believe that a person is supposed to be a certain way, it makes it hard to feel, and harder to act a different way. Religion tells us that gay men are sinners. If you are raised to believe that, and you know you are attracted to the same sex, it becomes ultra-difficult to physically act on your desire.

Your friend seems to have tried to test the straight waters, but he is acknowledging his true emotional and physical preference, and as his friend, you should support him. He isn't any different than he was before he told you, so don't hold the pressure of straight society against him.

We are in control of our own actions, but I believe that we are not always in control of our emotions. If a person is gay or straight in their heart and brain, that is something that I believe cannot be changed.

Whether they participate in any activity with a person of the same sex or not does not *prove* anything. People seek pleasure in many ways and a sexual act does not dictate our emotions for the other person. A gay man that never kisses another man is still gay, just like a straight woman that makes out with chicks at a bar is still straight. Embrace your friend and don't be afraid to learn about his experience as a gay man. It won't rub off, unless you both want it to.

Best of luck, remember that you matter most!

THE EGA TO ATTRACTION
Ms. Dumbbell Diva

"There is a guy at my gym that I have a huge crush on. I see him almost every time I am in there, and I want him to ask me out. He seems to be pretty dedicated to his workout while he is in the gym, so I am a little scared to interrupt him in his routine, and I am really afraid of asking him to meet me outside of the gym. What is a good way to approach a man or get him to ask me out?"

The difference between a fantasy and reality for a woman is dependent upon her ambition. By virtue of having a vagina you are entitled to a certain amount of leeway in approaching a man during his more isolated activities. You are well within your rights to interrupt this gentleman after one of his sets to ask about his diet. "Is vagina paleo?"

Chances are he has seen you and would totally do you, but he probably doesn't want to bother you or stare at you while you do your inner thigh workout. Just like your next pair of shoes, that man is waiting for you to own him. You may not be able to afford the shoes today, but you splurge because they were too cute to pass up. If this guy is as cute as you say, then you need to swallow your pride and treat yourself to his company. Ask him to join you for a smoothie after your workout, he will only decline if he has a valid excuse or a girlfriend, and even then it might not stop him.

After your workout you are as full of testosterone as you will ever be, so take advantage of that hormonal state to be bold and get your man. The more you think about that fantasy the easier it will be to keep it at arms length. You are going to have to know that you can have that man, and then you are going to have to act on that feeling.

Men appreciate a woman that will take a risk. You deserve to have the best of everything in your life, and if this guy is what you want, then you owe it to yourself to try. The shoes didn't jump into your shopping cart, and this guy won't jump into your bed until you pick him up and take him home. You are in the gym to work on your body, so add one more exercise to your routine the next time you see this beefcake, and pick up a date for the evening. It just might be the easiest lift you do that day, and it could lead to a much more fun kind of workout later on. Best of luck, remember that you matter most!

Ms. Cavewoman

"I have a really good boyfriend, but he lacks masculinity and that turns me off so much about him. He just isn't assertive. I could walk all over him. It is as if I am the man in the relationship when it comes to putting my foot down, making important decisions, and getting things done. We have been in public and guys will try to literally pull me away from him to get my number and he doesn't do anything! Can you give me some serious insight into how to make this work?"

I understand your desire to have a man that will "be a man". You are not alone in your belief that the man should take care of things like fixing stuff around the house as well as being assertive in showing that he loves you, and should protect you from these other men that find you desirable. Since we moved from the cave to the suburb, the traditional role of the man has been given a remix. We are no longer required to kill our food so that we can eat, and the man isn't supposed to beat his woman for burning the chicken.

Since the invention of the PlayStation, men require less and less of a woman, and they have been neglecting the basic man duties in order to finish their game of Madden. As a woman, it is a blessing and a curse. The de-masculization of our culture has allowed you to seek work instead of being tied up with an apron and childcare duties, but it has also created the sub-species of man called metrosexual and another variety called the good-for-nothing. A man back in the cave would not have stuck around after raping you to help raise the children or fix the air conditioner.

Your boyfriend has trust in your judgment and behaviors, and he hopes that you are deeply enough in love with him. He hopes you respect the relationship you both have built together. By not confronting a man that is pulling you away to get your phone number, he may be preventing a physical confrontation, or he may be testing you to see how you behave. The worst thing you can do is tell him to "man up" or that he is not a man, and you desire someone with more butch assertiveness. When you do that, he will more than likely shut down and not respond in the way you want.

What you need to do is watch him and praise his macho behaviors when they occur. By giving him reinforcement of an action you desire, you are letting him know you appreciate it, and he will do more things that get a good response from you. Be patient with the man as he transitions from dud to stud. It seems bad now, but look on the bright side; he isn't beating you or forcing you to have sex with him. He isn't fighting people out of his insecurity in your relationship. There isn't a lot of room in the relationship pants, so encourage him to put them on slowly. With both of you sharing a leg, hope that they don't split down the middle. Best of luck, remember that you matter most!

Ms. Right Now

"I could really use your help! I'm so confused. I met this guy about a week ago at a bar with friends. We really hit it off. We spent the whole night hanging out, and talked until the sunrise. It was incredible. We kissed a bit but nothing beyond that. The next day he called and we talked for about an hour. We have so much in common, and I was really excited about getting to know him better.

Sounds awesome, right? Well, when we talked on the phone he said that he wanted to take me out later that week (it was Sunday when we talked). He hasn't called me since. Today is Thursday. However, he did text "Hey, what's up?" a few minutes ago. Why bother calling and asking me out if you aren't going to call to make the date and are just going to send lame texts? What the hell?"

What you need to do is take a step back from the urban fairy tale you are creating for yourself and see things from a different perspective; his. You spent a night at a bar and an hour on the phone with a guy that won't give you the time of day now. I am sure that under the influence of a few cosmos and sexual tension, you thought you had met the one, but in reality you have just been entertained and entertaining for someone else. Like every romantic comedy made ever, the guy that likes you is the guy that makes time for you. Do not trust a text message. Any man that abbreviates his time with you is not worth you burning calories over. Instead of worrying about what he is doing, go be productive. Live your life until you find a guy that wants to take time out of his day to be with you, and doesn't stop until you want him to. Guys will use people to take up time in their life. You were there to play with last week, and if he needs you again he will pull your card when the time comes. Don't fault him for using his time wisely, and don't fall into his trap, unless you don't mind being his seat filler. You are smarter than that, right? Right? Instead of the fairy tale you were creating, slow down and read between the lines. It is too easy to see things that aren't really there when we are all lusty and lonely, so look at his actions to guide your expectations. Best of luck, remember that you matter most!

Mr. Odd Man Out

"I went to the bar the other day and I was watching a girl that I wanted to approach. Just before I did I saw another girl come over, run her hands across her breasts, and give her a kiss on lips. Nothing about the girl or her friend gave off any gay vibe. It is not the first time I have seen girls playing with girls, but why do they do that?"

I often find myself at local drinking establishments; it is a side effect of not having a television at home. I also have seen girls acting frisky with one another. I decided to take your question straight to the source. While watching a game this week, I sat next to two young ladies sipping on crown and cokes (in 16 oz. cups). I started with the simple who's and what's and then I asked if they were dating each other. They said that they were roommates, but not a couple. I noticed that as the drinks were refilled they got touchier with each other.

When I asked them why they tease each other, they said that playing with each other keeps them from being naughty with a predator such as me. These girls gave just one reason why girls play with girls, others are for attention from men and other women, or they might be a really loving couple. Just because the girls are keeping their hands to themselves doesn't mean they won't be willing to lend you one.

As I continued to chat with these girls, I began to understand their reasoning. I told them that one of the reasons I play with myself is to keep myself safe from women like them. I almost envied their ability to play as they do, because two straight guys could never get away with caressing each other as an excuse to behave.

The next time you see girls being frisky, don't be afraid to approach. If they are gay, or they tell you they are, you didn't waste too many calories. If they are just on a play date, then you can jump into the sandbox and play along if they feel like sharing. Best of luck, remember that you matter most!

Mr. Chicken or Fish?

"I am attending a wedding this weekend, and I am going stag. I was wondering if you have had any advice about wedding hookups, since there is the *Wedding Crashers* stereotype that weddings are the place to get lucky. What can I do to improve my chances of getting a girl to say "I do"?"

I, too, have wondered about the validity of the wedding stereotype. I have been attending more and more weddings recently as my friends pair off to mate for life or death do them part. I have mostly gone single to the weddings and I have always gone home alone, but not from a lack of trying. The last wedding I attended, I traveled with another friend and was rooming with a young lady that shared her perspective on the myth with us.

She stated that the stereotype of emotions are true; meaning that the girls that are at the wedding are thinking about their special day in the future and how much they want to be loved for life. Some are all ooey-gooey inside. How that translates into a sexual appetite is different for every woman. Being at a wedding is a great place to do some experimenting. As a single man, you are able to make your time valuable, or you can be a wallflower all night, hugging the open bar.

The ceremony is a good place to observe what you have to work with. Sitting in the row just behind the family is a great place to see everyone that comes in and who they are there for. This will help the conversation later when you approach whomever with "So how do you know <u>insert bride or groom</u>"?

The reception is nothing more than a glorified petting zoo. Everyone will be grouped according to their breeds and availability to be stroked or petted. You will more than likely be at a table with other singles or people your age. During the early part of the reception, pay close attention to the people that spend their time at the bar.

The women that are bellying up may be there to loosen up their moral garters, or they may be there to drown away their sorrows about always being a bridesmaid and never the bride. If there is a single woman at your table, chances are that you may have a head start at a connection since you are both alone and about to get wasted. Within the first few minutes of dialogue with her, make sure that you bring up a funny story with you and whoever invited you, and ask her why she decided to come alone, not "Are you single?"

When the dancing begins, you have two objectives. The first is to dance with the oldest or most physically handicapped of all the guests. People will see you doing your good deed and will be warmed by your compassion, as well as impressed by your bravery. This will let any potential unknown suitor for your services come to the surface. The second is to ask the cutie downing the gin and sprites to dance. She may say no at first, but she will come around when her song comes on.

Continue to work the room using your petting zoo map. The single girls flock together, usually by a water source or cheese tray. When you approach, introduce yourself and wait until a break in the conversation to single out the one you want to pet. You can't scare one of the animals that or the group will attack.

Once you know who you are most interested in, then find her married friend (they all have one). Ask her to dance; she will say yes since husbands don't dance. Now you are part of a sick foreplay game for married couples at weddings. During your dance you are going to ask about the status of your desirable. If she is single and she thinks you are cute the married girl will introduce you. If the answer is no, then she will tell you she has a boyfriend. Accept whatever she says as truth. If more than one slow song is played in a row, it is just about closing time.

Round up the lush that rejected you earlier and tell her that you have waited long enough for her to come ask you to dance, and go cut a rug. Be charming, and invite her to the after party back at the hotel bar. Yes means yes, no means no. You are half way home at that point either way. Don't forget a condom, and don't mention it. Best of luck, remember that you matter most!

Ms. Best of Both Worlds

"My issue is that when I give it up, if there is a spark between us, a connection, and the sex was spine tingling, I get emotional and want more than just physical stuff. The bad thing that I do is telling these guys about my feelings after a few weeks and totally run them off. I do have guys that want to know about me and they want me to be their girl, but I have no attraction to them. If I am just going to have a fling, how do I not get so attached?"

You are not alone in your situation. The stereotype is that women have a hard time separating their emotions from sex. Women are taught from birth that sex equals love, so of course you are going to have lovey-dovey feelings after some yummy sex. With oxytocin and society influencing you, it becomes hard to resist building intimacy with a sex partner. Unfortunately for women everywhere, men are taught the opposite (at least the ones out having casual sex). Your reward for being brave enough to share your body with a man is often no return call and unmet expectations for the near future. There is a real simple way to ensure you get what you want out of the man emotionally, but it does not happen overnight.

If you are able to hold out until you and the

man develop rapport and intimacy outside of the bedroom, there is a chance he will start investing some emotional energy in you. This is not about slut shaming or telling you that he won't buy the cow if the milk is free. A man that is only looking for a short-term hookup will not take the time to get to know a girl, because he isn't interested in that. A good way to tell is if he only wants to meet you when it is dark outside, or one or both of you is drunk when you get together. Any man worth having you as a sexual partner will wait at least a month before he stops calling.

Game playing isn't something I recommend, but a man is like a roach. If you leave food out it will come out at night and eat, but he's gone in the morning. If you keep your house clean for a while, only a persistent critter is going to keep coming back. Once you decide that a man has stuck around long enough, then BAM! Close that Venus-mantrap of yours around him, and you have yourself a boyfriend. In the mean time have hot sex with an asshole if you want, but as long as you have a potential partner to keep your mind on, sex can just be sex without the emotional investment. Partnership is a numbers game. Enjoy your Netflix and chills, just make sure that you are also meeting other potential partners during the day. Best of luck, remember that you matter most!

Mr. Young Jedi

"How can I convince someone that I am the right person for them to be with? I have been dating this girl, she has every trait I want in a future wife. The only problem is that she doesn't feel the same way. I have tried everything to show her that she should see things my way, and I think she is scared of how powerful we can be together. What else can I say or do to get through to this girl?"

The force may not be strong within you yet. Bending the will of others takes years of practice and a string of failures before you achieve the potential to brainwash another person to do your will, grasshopper. That said; it is not impossible to input subliminal messages in the mind of another person to achieve a desired outcome. You say you have done everything, and maybe you have. That may have been your downfall. The optimal approach to sustaining a potential life partner is a slow bleeding of important desires from you about the planning of your union.

I have read every Harry Potter book. Each one builds suspense to the moment that Harry and "he who shall not be named" square off head to head, and who is going to end up with Hermione. Like every one that has read the books or watched the movies, we are emotionally invested in the characters, and we are dying to know how they will end up. Had we picked up the last book without reading any of the first six, we might enjoy the story, but we wouldn't care half as much because we didn't put in the work to earn the payoff.

When you throw out how sprung you are on this girl, and then you give out the ending to your story before she even buys the book you have to understand that you just spoiled the journey for her. Beyond that, you place a burden of expectation upon the courtship. Now when you do something stupid (which inevitably we all do) she will be thinking, "Do I want to be married to that?", or "Is that what I want in my children's father?" Instead, she should be saying "That is so cute, you messed up and I can deal with that because I don't want to hold it against you in the future since I don't know what the future holds". In other words, you give up your get out of jail free card.

Maybe you can still pull the emergency brake on the relationship coaster you are on. Let her know that you don't mean to hold her to these expectations that you voiced, that you are just passionate about her and that you intend to devote your energy to creating a positive relationship for the two of you. The words "One day at a time," or "I have enjoyed getting to know you," come to mind as possible options.

See how that goes, and if the flame is no longer lit for one of you, it means that the relationship is over for the both of you. All you can do is hope that absence makes the heart grow fonder. You shouldn't spend time barking up the wrong tree, because there is a thin line between love and hate. There is an even thinner line between admiring from afar, stalking, and a restraining order.

That goes for the phone/email/texting/IM as well, whatever you kids are doing to communicate these days. My personal strategy for success depends on Jedi mind tricks too, but no means no. There has to be an active dialogue for you to implant positive thoughts. If the door is shut, there is no picking the lock (literally and figuratively). There are millions of other women that would be happy to share the same dream you have for this girl, and you would let them. You just haven't met them yet. Best of luck, remember that you matter most!

Mr. Strike Out

"How can I let a girl know that I like her without sounding like all I want is sex? I am trying to meet a woman that wants more than just a one-night stand."

The first thing you can do to find a woman that will not think you only want sex is to get out of the night club. If you are in a place where they only serve alcohol, then the women are more likely to believe that you, too, are only selling one thing. Take your game outdoors to a public event or even indoors during the daytime. The chances are greater of meeting the same girl from the club but getting a different result if you meet her on a neutral playing field.

You can stack the deck in your favor by selecting an event or place that brings people together with similar interests (hobby, certain aisles in a bookstore). The women are not as on their guard as they are in a club. You can be the same loveable guy in the book store that you are in the club, and the girl will actually listen to what you have to say because her mind isn't on rejection first, as it is in the bar.

Win her over with your intellect, and you may have made more than just a friend for one night. Here is a Dr. Ethan Gregory original tip guaranteed to work that I promise you haven't heard elsewhere; you have more courage in the club when you are tipsy, so why not try it in the bookstore? Have a drink before you leave your house, eat a pb&j, and brush your teeth before you go. By the time you get to the daytime meat market, you will be loose enough to strike up a conversation but have no outward sign of intoxication. If that doesn't work, at least you have an early start for happy hour. Best of luck, remember that you matter most!

Mr. Heart Shaped Hero

"I have been interested in a girl for a while now. I have never asked her on a date before, although we go out in the same group of friends every now and then. She has said that she hates Valentines Day, but I was thinking that Valentines Day would be a great first date. Should I go for it, or wait for another time to ask her out?"

Girls hate Valentines Day because it reminds them of all the reasons they are not in a relationship, and all the people that ever lied to them and broke their heart. It is a holiday for couples, and women get enough grief throughout the year for not being in a relationship. Valentines Day for these women is like the first time we as guys find hair on our ears. We immediately feel undesirable and that no one will ever love us now that we are turning into werewolves.

We can all agree that like every other holiday, consumerism has taken over, but as a person that makes a living off of other people's misery and uncertainty, Valentines Day is my Easter. The ides of February bring hope for every lonely person that someone will appreciate them for who they are, and make that 14th special for them. So yes, this girl has hated V-day, but you have a chance to make her change her mind, because any girl would have a hard time rejecting someone asking for a date on that day (that said, even I have been rejected for a V-day date). Yes, you are playing into her insecurity, and yes, that is somewhat of a douche thing to do; but you are who matters here. So no, I don't have a problem with that.

When you put yourself and V-day in the same thought, remember that you are associating yourself with all that V-day means- romance, hope, and the potential for true love. The important thing for you to do is to not go overboard, because it is a first date. There is already a lot of pressure on that, and having V-day complicate things doesn't make it any easier. Use your collected memories of this girl to figure out what she likes, and try to include that in the date. Make it a double feature, active and passive. Have an activity that she will enjoy, (not paintball) then time for you to talk in a place that doesn't sing happy birthday to the customers.

Stay away from any set menu places because you are not a couple yet. I recommend cooking her dinner at your place after your day activity (note to self, clean up). Have an early dinner and then take her out for drinks and dessert. Go to the place ahead of time and give the bartender $50 bucks. Tell the guy that you are bringing a date later, and you want the drinks and snacks to be "on the house" (yes, this works). Leave the change as a tip. If things go well you will have restored her faith in men, V-day, and the two of you might get hit with cupid's arrow. After I was rejected for my V-date, I ended up taking a girl for a salsa lesson, and we had a great time as friends. It wasn't busy and would be a great intimacy builder. My date ended up being asexual, but you might fare better. Best of luck, remember you matter most!

Mr. Buy You a Drink

"When I am out in a bar or a social gathering, I notice that the girls I talk to seem to lose interest in me soon after I approach them. When I meet them I introduce myself, buy them a drink, and I think I have a good personality. Why is it that the only ones that seem to keep the conversation going are the ones I lose interest in?"

As long as women have been allowed in drinking establishments for anything other than working as a floor sweeper or a lady of the night, men have been buying drinks for them. It might seem like a harmless gesture and an act of chivalry, but I think between the two of us, we know that the true meaning of supplying a woman with a drink is to help her lose the inhibition she had to talk to you in the first place.

During my social research days (going out a lot) I noticed the same women working new men every 15 minutes to get a free drink if they wanted. These drink divas are often pretty, but shallow as a puddle in the city on a hot day. When you play into the drink cliché you are actually doing more harm than good for your future with that woman. You aren't buying a guy stranger a drink before you start talking to him about the game, and you shouldn't do it for a girl stranger either.

When you use money to provide something to a stranger (even a drink) you are establishing yourself as a person that uses money to try and get your way, or provide for the woman. When you trick your cash for a girl in a bar they will milk you for it, and then leave with the guy they wanted from the start. Before you buy that next appletini, keep your money in your pocket and pull out that good personality instead. When you have created a rapport with the girl, then you can split rounds.

Using this method will weed out the gold diggers, and you can then survey your options from there. If you are lucky, you might end up with a two for one special of looks and personality. Anything other than that and you are just happy hour for a selfish lady. Best of luck, remember that you matter most!

Ms. Hope Holder

"How can women know that a guy is interested in us? About four weeks ago I had one of my co-workers give this guy my number, he then came to me, and asked how old I was. It turns out that he is 13 years older than I am. He said he was flattered but he only dates women in their thirties and forties. Just recently he has been talking to me more and more, he hasn't called me but we always seem to head out of the building at the same time, and he is almost always behind me when we pull out of the parking garage. I just want to know if he is interested in me. Do you think I should just ask him? Hopefully you can help me."

This man in particular is not interested in you. When you talked a month ago he stated that he doesn't date women your age, but what he meant was that he doesn't want to date you specifically. If you leave the building when your work day is done it seems to make sense that he might be behind you in the line of cars leaving work. He might be a stalker, but he is not a suitor. This gentleman doesn't feel any pressure or anxiety in talking to you because he believes that he has made it crystal clear that he isn't interested in pursuing a passionate and romantic relationship with you. He is playing the friendly flirt card, and you should not call his bluff, because you will lose. I am sorry to be so blunt but it is the truth.

Guys can be dicks sometimes. He already set an emotional boundary for your relationship, yet he is now coming around to get some satisfaction and emotional support from you, because he knows that he can get away with it. It may feel good to have him paying attention to you, but understand this; it will never advance past the water cooler. He may try and do you some day, but that will be all.

To answer your question about when a man really likes a woman, you will find that a man will make any excuse to get near the woman they like. They will often bring them tokens of their affection, and they will never pass up an opportunity to go on a date. A man that talks to you may seem nice, but know that they will put their penis in you way before they put their trust in you. If you have the "balls" to do it, asking a man if they are interested in dating you will almost always get you the answer; it just may not be the answer that you are looking for. Anything other than a 100% yes means that he isn't looking for a commitment. If you want more, do not allow yourself to be used for less. Best of luck, remember that you matter most!

Mr. Excess Baggage

"I have not been dating for a long while, mostly because I have been occupied with other things, and I haven't felt the urge to get out in the scene that exists for singles. I am getting my nerve up again, but I am two months away from relocation for work to another state. Is it wrong to start dating someone just for a time filler before I move away?"

Most questions I answer have me telling people to be selfish about their desires and to go for what they want. In your case I am thinking you should think about the other person while you try and meet your needs. For easy sex the "I am only in town for one night" works, especially at hotel bars, but the line "I am only in town for two months" might not produce the same success rate. All single people (and most married people) get the itch to have hot random sex or an intense emotional attachment from time to time. If you want to have a mini relationship, then by all means do it; just make sure that you let the unlucky lady know early that you are leaving on a jet plane, and don't know when you'll be back again.

If she is smart, she will appreciate the concept of a fun few months to feel good. Whatever you do, don't hide the fact that you are gonzo soon just to lock a girl down for a short time. Then you become that creep that disappears right when emotions get strong. Best of luck, remember that you matter most!

Ms. All Inclusive

"I have been planning a trip with a group of friends for some time, and as the date gets closer, people have dropped out, except me and one of my guy friends in the group. When it was a big group there was no problem with splitting rooms, we rented a large villa. Now that it is just he and I, I don't know if I should go. I have a boyfriend, and I don't know what he would think about me rooming with a guy for one week. My boyfriend can't go for work reasons, and full disclosure, I am attracted to this friend, should I just bail out or keep the reservations as they are?"

Group trips are great, but you might have a better time with a guy friend than you would if there were more opinions on what to do and when. Fun in the sun does not have to be full of sexual tension- in fact, the two of you can be good wingmen as long as you can handle being tipsy and cohabitating with someone you kind of like for a week in paradise.

The friend should be under no pressure to cancel the trip, it is his vacation too. It could be that you are worried about what your boyfriend thinks because you know in your heart that something might happen given the circumstances. If you are feeling pre-cheating guilt then maybe you should think about why that is, and why you have the boyfriend you do. This could be a great opportunity to break one relationship off and start a new one with your soon to be roommate. A man can't help but think about sex when he stays anywhere near a woman, but it doesn't mean that he will attack you. He will be paying close attention to how you act, and if you want to give him an opening, believe that he might take it.

When you get back, there are going to be rumors anyway, so they can either be squashed, or you can earn the water cooler chatter. I think you should let this be an exercise in trust for you and your boyfriend. If something does happen, establish the rules ahead of time and take it to your grave. What happens on vacation needs to stay on vacation, or you need to be willing to make the switch. Best of luck, remember that you matter most!

Ms. Subliminal Messaging

"I have been meeting men online for the past year. I have been on several dates, but nothing serious has come from the guys I meet on the personal ad sites. These men say they want to start a family and find a good woman, but they don't hang around long. They can see from my profile and pictures that I am attractive and that I am a good mother as well. Why are they rejecting me?"

Men online are exactly like the men you see on the street. They will check you out, they may even ask you out, but when you don't sleep with them on the first date, they might forget your phone number. My doctoral dissertation was about dating and mate selection, and I found out something shocking during my research. Men don't waste their time on hot mommies that don't put out. I know, that sounds crazy, but it is a sad reality for all the MILFs of the world. Putting your profile online is great for making it easy for men to reject you. Another sad reality of online dating is that men don't have to be picky.

A man with nothing to do might as well take you on a date, because his chance of getting a little warm n' wet is higher than normal because there is more competition between women for that pool of men online. If you aren't giving out sexual tapas, you might miss out on a man who just got an early bird special from his date the previous day. Men are like moths, and you should treat us like one. You are giving out way too much info before you even meet Mr. Potential. Women tend to go overboard with the personal ads. Do your future a favor and start with a blank page/profile/personal ad. Your ad is a pitch-black room right now. What is most important for a man to know about you should go on the page, and that's it.

The moth-man will be drawn to that like a bright light. What you think is important is not what he will think is important. Your ad should say available and hot.

Saying yes to having a child is not the same as putting the family album on the personal ad. Women that have in the first few lines of their profile "My kids are my world," or "My child is the most important thing in my life," are the women that will have their profiles on there the longest.

A man already knows that children are a priority, and no mom is going to write, "My kids are the last thing I want to deal with," or "I choose men over my children every time." What women advertise in those ads is that "A man will never get the affection they want from me," even if that isn't what they mean. The women that have their child on their profile pics and say they are there for dating are only going to get creeps and spammers filling their inbox. Treat yourself like an onion and let the dudes you meet in person peel back the layers. Best of luck, remember that you matter most!

Ms. More Bang for Your Buck

"I am back on the market for the first time in a long time. I signed on to a dating service and I have lots of men asking me for dates. I am meeting guys during the week, and I have seen a few of them a couple times. I feel like I am a player because I am dating several guys at one time. Is it wrong to be dating more than one man at a time? When do I let the others know about each other?"

Welcome back in the game! You seem to have come off the bench with some pep in your step. Don't worry about the overabundance of available men, run through them like a knife through butter. The men never have to know about each other, and trust me, the men don't care when it comes to the initial stages of dating. A man is doing the same thing, he is just not telling you about it. Dating services are good for creating a bigger pool of applicants, and it is important to start weeding them out. Profiles online often mask true looks and issues that only a face to face meeting will bring out. Don't feel bad about dating more than one person at a time or sleeping with all of them; only when you decide to commit to one would you become come a naughty girl for keeping up the others.

Give yourself a three-week date maximum with each guy. Have one date and start watching the possessiveness in between dates. If he calls the day before a date to ask you out, minus that guy. If he texts you or calls more than a few times each day he is a bit clingy and could turn into one of those stalking, abusive boyfriends that you swore you would never date again. If after three dates you are still interested then take the profile off until the guy blows it. Stop interacting with the other guys and they will get the hint. Best of luck, remember that you matter most!

Mr. How Low Can You Go?

"I frequent a bar weekly, and I have started to notice the same people there when I am. There are ladies I would like to meet and possibly date, but I am afraid that if I go for one, I might be seen and then miss one of the others. How can I keep a low profile and try to meet girls at the same club?"

It is a nice feeling to go where everybody knows your name, but is a sad feeling to gain the reputation of creepy dude that hits on all the local girls. As you sip from your cocktail and scan the room for potential partners, your first move should be to hit the group of girls. When girls pair up it is to the benefit of the causal conversation because you can chat up the group and not look like you are hitting on either one. If a young lady has her eye on you while you are in the company of others, don't be surprised. A man that is in the company of other women becomes more attractive as a potential mate.

If you strike out with the group, look confident and wear a smile back to your barstool. Go for a free-range chick with your second attempt later on, or on another night. If you can remember names of the locals you interact with before, saying hello when you see them again invites them to initiate conversation with you and shows that you are friendly to the silent-but-judging onlookers. Do not be afraid to utilize the help. Make sure you tip well each time and be on a first name basis with the bartenders. You never know who plays matchmaker behind the scenes.

The worst thing you can do is try to hit for the cycle in one night. When you spread out the at-bats you will find your average goes up over the course of a season. If things go horribly wrong ,retain your dignity and your place at the bar, let her be the one to find another watering hole. Best of luck, remember that you matter most!

Ms. Rejection

"How do I tell someone that I am not interested in dating them? I have people approach me all the time, but they are not what I am looking for. I do not like hurting feelings, but I do not want to lead these guys on. Is there a way to let them down gently?"

If a man asks you out, there is no obligation to actually go out with him. Men that ask you on a date are like a trial for a magazine. You might not want the year's subscription, but if you accept the three free issues, you usually end up getting charged for the whole year, and by that time no amount of complaining will get you out of the subscription without some drama. Asking a woman on a date is hard, but we didn't invest any emotion in asking you out. If you say no, it is like saying yes for someone else. Just be honest and say that you do not want to go out with him. He won't be hurt; he should be relieved that you sent him towards destiny.

When you are thinking about hurt feelings, it is your own guilt that hurts, and that shouldn't be that painful since you should care enough about yourself and your time not to waste it on someone that doesn't light your fire. Love yourself, and tell the gentleman that you appreciate his offer and interest but there will be no date with you now or in the future, thank you and good day. That will do it. When you reject you accept (yourself) and deflect (compromising your values). Now take time and reflect. Best of luck, remember that you matter most!

Mr. Nice Guy

"When I am out, anytime that I meet a girl I want to sleep with, I can hold a good conversation, but when I ask her home with me I don't know what to say or do. I consider myself a nice guy, and I don't want to offend the person I am with in case I see them again. I feel like I am right on the edge of getting a yes, but I fumble over my words when I say that I want them to come home with me. Is there a good line to use or technique that will help me get over the hump?"

This reminds me of a story from back in the day. I was once on a cruise to the Bahamas, around 1:00am, I am heading back to the cabin to go to bed (I value sleep) when I see one of my friends entertaining the company of a much older woman. I mosey on over to the bar and ask him how things are going. He tells me that the woman is here with her husband, who had gone to bed for the evening many hours ago. He doesn't gamble, he doesn't drink, and she is a drinking, gambling, night owl. As it was getting late in the night, I understood why this woman was still at the bar chatting up a man half her age.

I told my friend that it was time to become aggressive if he wanted to engage in anything indecent with this lady. She was giving him the opportunity to help her make a bad decision. If he asked her to join him in his cabin or anywhere else more private, she most likely would have obliged. She wanted attention. She wanted to feel attractive, and she wanted to have that tingle of passion that she may not have had since her husband turned into a prude. I watched from afar as he got her up from the bar and began to walk towards the room, but she stopped at a poker machine and began to play. That was where he messed up.

He should have created a situation where she saw the option to return with him or to go to her own room. She stalled, and he never made the advance she was waiting for. Eventually, she returned to her cabin. The moral of the story is that sometimes you have to assert yourself. The married lady was dangling her lure out in front of him, but he just nibbled at the bait. That woman wanted his young strong body for her pleasure, but he was just passive enough to miss the pleasure cruise. Being a nice guy like he was, I know he didn't want to offend her or miss his opportunity. Aggressive suggestion would have gotten him laid, but that isn't part of the nice guy repertoire.

If you coax out your inner bad boy in select

situations, you will become more successful. There is no downside to being bold in that kind of situation. Whether it is closing time at your local pub and you are chatting up a potential mate, or you are in an exotic location with a woman that is looking for a memorable secret to keep, you can succeed where others fail using a confident close the deal statement. If she seems the type of girl that needs a little boost try "I am going (where you want to take her), come with me," in a confident voice right against her earlobe, establishing touch as you say it. She will know why, and she will admire the confidence you show in your desire for her.

For a more lighthearted approach use this Ethan Gregory staple, "let's have a slumber party". That line is a safer version with more ambiguity built in. Who doesn't want to have a slumber party full of laughter, sex, and fun? The most basic of all take me home tonight's is "Are you ready to go to my place?" That line implies that the choice has already been made (which it has) and can keep tension low and expectations high. The key is in the delivery. Confidence begets coitus, but no means no. Best of luck, remember that you matter most!

Ms. Kid in a Candy Shop

"I have an annual convention this week. The event is three days long with people from all over the state. I am a single intelligent female, and I am in a field with mostly men. If I want to hook up, how should I go about it without making it totally awkward for both of us?"

I, too, attend these kinds of events from time to time, and I see where there is both opportunity to be sly and enjoy the benefits of casual companionship, and the chance to ruin a career by picking someone that will kiss and tell. There are some good rules to go by for these situations, and they can be applied to most out of town for multi-day events (cruises, weddings, etc.). The most important day of your convention is the first day. Do yourself a favor and only observe if you can help it. Guys will be watching you to see who you talk with, and most men are afraid of confrontation. They will write you off as taken if they see you chatting up some strange man. Your opportunity to shine will be in the small groups or workshops, or whatever you call them in your field.

Make sure that you raise your hand to answer a question. That will guarantee that you have some spotlight. By the end of the day, you should know which men catch your eye. If you want to make the most of the trip, just go to another hotel's bar for the night. Day two is your day to work your way down the list of potential partners. Chat up the ones you really like and determine which are off limits by two degrees of separation or less. Don't do anyone that might one day be your boss. Your best bet is to pick the youngest good-looking guy in the room, because he is most likely to be unmarried, horny, and will have less liability in case he does blab about that thing you do with your hips.

Try to distance yourself from your co-workers as to not raise suspicion when you go to the hotel room. Be prepared to hurry in the morning in case you pull an all-nighter. One time I had to have a friend bring his clothes from the day before so I didn't have the same outfit two consecutive days. Show up for the final day, and completely ignore the gent for the rest of the time you are there. Go home with confidence that you got the most out of your experience. Most people will only go home with free pens. Best of luck, remember that you matter most!

Mr. Take the Easy Way Out

"I am going to a conference this weekend, and I will be seeing people that I know from other conferences. There is a woman that I know for sure is going to be there, and we almost hooked up at the last conference. I think that I could do it this time, but I might see someone new there, and I don't want to be tied down or look involved. Is there a way to do both?"

Any time we take ourselves out of our comfort zone or routine, there is a thrill of the unknown to drive us to be naughty. Going to a conference means like-minded people and the opportunity to network for business and pleasure. It sounds like you laid some groundwork already with this girl, but you want to keep those options open. You need to make a decision on the first day to either find a new target or stick with a sure thing. Otherwise, you are extending yourself beyond what you are capable of doing and you might lose both opportunities, leaving you with just the real reason you are at this thing in the first place, work.

To avoid that, think about why you want to be sexual with this woman. If you think she is hot, then of course do her and make an effort to forget whatever else is out there. If you are not interested in her and just want to lose some baby making weight, let me give you some advice from personal experience. I spent most of my younger days experiencing sex and at times playing a numbers game. As a mature adult, I am more of a connoisseur. I am drawn to unique challenges and intriguing women to keep things interesting.

The lesson is that sometimes dry dick can be more fulfilling than wet dick. If you think that the sex is easy to get, it might not mean anything to you, so you should let it go. Let some other douche bag that needs to get his numbers up mercy fuck this poor woman. Have some strength of character and feel good about choosing not to devalue a woman with your cheap sex.

Go find an intriguing woman and you will have a much better story to tell than the vagina that fell onto your lap. If there is nothing else worth trying for at this conference, and you feel like being a sexual enabler, then go ahead and knock it out of the park, who am I to judge? Best of luck, remember that you matter most!

Ms. Talk to the Hand

"I am a married woman, and when I go out, guys often hit on me. When I show them my ring or tell them I am married some still try and get my number and talk to me. They say things like "Is your husband married to you?" and "I'm not trying to date your husband." How can I get my point across without hurting their feelings? I don't want to be mean, but I don't want to be bothered anymore."

Being a woman is hard work. You pick out nice outfits to work in, you work hard all day, and then when you go out to relax you are forced to deal with douche bags hitting on you. In pre-marital days that was all well and good, but now that you have a happy husband waiting at home for you, guys wanting to get to know you is flattering but can quickly turn to annoyance as they keep up the persistent routine. Instead of being ear-raped all night while you try and be nice, I have some simple statements for you to use the next time someone won't take no for an answer.

While minding your next martini, if a man comes up to you and asks to buy you a drink kindly refuse. If the caveman in the suit doesn't go away, the next time he utters a word in your direction, tell him that you are not interested in getting to know him, and that you are there to enjoy your drink alone.

If this man decides to play puppy dog, ignore him completely. Do not entertain any part of his retort or inquiry as to why you choose to drink alone. Another pro-active rejection is to say that you will take a free drink if the man wants to throw away his money, but you are not going to communicate with him. You are a big girl; make up your own pro-active rejections that fit your personality.

The most important lesson for you to learn is that a man (or anyone that wants something from another person) doesn't always stop seeking his or her goal without a clear understanding that it isn't happening. Being nice is fine, you don't have to smack them in the face as you dump a drink in his lap to get the point across. The one thing you cannot do is make your rejection about someone else. When you say that you have a boyfriend, husband, or you are meeting friends in a bit, you are taking your power away and giving it to the guy trying to do you. Short of saying you have HIV and an active herpes flare up, a person wanting to be inside you doesn't need to know you are married or in a relationship. Plenty of naughty boys and girls have ruined that excuse for the rest of us.

When you say you are married, you are saying, "I really want to talk to you and I may even want to have all kinds of sex with you, but I might get in trouble with my husband afterwards." Don't expect that to keep away a predator that wants to steal your virtue. Telling them that you are not going to talk to them because you don't want to is only rude in girl talk. A man will respect that and might even buy you a drink for being honest. Flashing your wedding ring to a guy in a bar is a silly move. Don't forget you are in a bar; this is his hunting grounds, not yours.

Be direct, and you can enjoy your drink and remain faithful to your husband without being rude. You are doing him a favor by letting him move on quickly to the next not-so-prepared married woman. "No thank you, I prefer to be alone," is enough to make your intentions clear. If someone doesn't respect your wishes, then feel free to get ignorant. Best of luck, remember that you matter most!

Ms. Same Script Different Cast

"I have a person in my night school class that I have known for about one year now. During a recent conversation, he told me that he is now single because his girlfriend left him. They had been together for seven years and she dumped him because he would not marry her. I am interested in him, and want to ask him out, but he hasn't shown any interest. Is he just shy, or is he still hurting from his break up? Should I make a move to ask him out?"

I appreciate the idea that people can change, and it is true that we act differently around people that know us in a variety of ways. You know this guy as an enjoyable person to be around, and from your perspective he seems like a good catch. You are an optimist and that is so cute. Let's look at some plain truths. This gentleman just got dumped, and he is thinking that it is not his fault. He is the victim in his mind, and trust me, he may be hurt, but he is thinking about one thing only; stranger sex. You could be that, but believe that there is no rebound here. This guy is a compete air ball. He dated a woman for seven years without even getting engaged.

This man doesn't have clothes from that long ago, and you think that you have a shot at everlasting love? You don't. Go ahead and have that hook up if you want, but I don't think he is super interested if he has not made a move on you yet. Of all the men in the world I would suggest you put him on the bottom of the list.

This person obviously has commitment issues, you deserve better. Keep your clear of drama and when you finish your schooling, find a stranger that you might one day settle down with. You don't need a person that thinks he might settle for you. Best of luck, remember that you matter most!

Mr. Maytag Repairman

"I met a girl at the club the other night while out with friends. She was sultry and frisky when we first interacted. Throughout the course of the night ,she changed from hot to cold. If we were dancing she would be as exotic and freaky as could be, then she would go quiet, bite her nails, and pay little attention to me. I didn't ever know what she wanted and I was afraid to make a move. How do you deal with these on/off girls? Is it ever possible to keep the switch on hot?"

Throughout history men have labeled women with a stereotype of not being able to make decisions. All men hate it when a question is answered with "I don't know, where do you want to go?" What we do wrong is label it as them not having an opinion on anything, when that is not the case. They may not care about where you eat, but they do care about slut shaming and earning a reputation.

Much like any air conditioner, a woman in the club runs on coolant. The AC unit uses Freon and a woman in the club runs on Grey Goose martinis, vodka/red bulls, and gin & tonics. Both create a comfortable situation in which to have a good time. If your girl was full of coolant then she may have been at full blast when you met her. She was loosey-goosey, letting her natural fun self come out, and you helped to make her feel that way with little compliments and showing her that she is desirable.

As her buzz ran out so did her letting it all hang out attitude. She became aware of her behavior. She may have seen her friends looking at the two of you and got insecure, or she could have remembered that she had a boyfriend. Either way, it is only a matter of time before she completely sputters out on you. She must have liked you and your company if she tried to keep you interested, but if a woman at any moment begins to act out of character from how you first met her, it is because they have made a decision to pull back on the reins. Her choices are hers to make and live with. If she doesn't say anything about why she pulls back assume she is conflicted- or on drugs- and you have two options.

When you are face to face with this situation again, tell her you like her. If she responds kindly, give her a little peck on the lips. If she tries to hit you then you can exercise option two, which is to cut your losses and forget about Dr. Jekyll & Ms. Hyde. There are other less conflicted women that want to enjoy your company.

If you kiss her and she doesn't run away or call security it means that she was waiting for you to make a move (which you did). Some girls are so old fashioned/conservative that they are never going to give you an obvious green light, which means that you have to be brave on occasion, run a yellow light before it turns red. If you are brave enough, it might pay off. Hopefully you have been reading the signals right, without being disrespectful.

If she is ambivalent about your respectful approach, tell her you don't mean to offend her, and you have enjoyed her time tonight, exchange numbers, and tell her you will be in touch. She could be having an off night, let her be and see how she is in the daylight. We as men are often overestimating the attraction women have for us. You can tell her that you want to kiss her if you are really unsure.

Many women enjoy a little make out session, but no woman likes being mouth-raped by a pushy dude. Be respectful as possible. Instead of a hot/cold girl you might end up with a cool hot chick. As with anything that requires consent, we want to make sure that we are respecting boundaries. If you can tell your girl is on the drunker side of tipsy, it's not worth risking your reputation on what might be her inability to make a clear decision. Consent is just as sexy as an impromptu make out session, so if you can't be sure, settle for exchanging numbers and tell her that you want to spend some time with her in the daylight, then walk away. Best of luck, remember that you matter most!

Mr. Love in All the Wrong Places

"I am going on a business trip to Tokyo next week, and I am excited about being in Asia because I have always had a thing for Asian women. I am interested in hiring the services of an escort for the duration of the trip. Is it worth the money, or should I try something different with my time?"

Lucky you, coming over to the Far East. I can tell you first hand that the experience of living in Asia will ruin your fetish for exotic beauties of the orient. I am never one to tell someone what they should or shouldn't do outright, but let me give you some strong advice. I see men all the time that are accompanied by professionals. They are living the dream by having a young thing on their arm at the bar, but under the surface, there is a hard truth about the interaction.

One person does not care about the other, and that makes it just a tad awkward to watch. It can be gross to see a sad looking girl on her phone waiting for some old expat to order their lunch. As a single male that is aware of his own sexuality and with extra time on his hands during lonely moments, I understand the urge to hire professional help to get your oil changed. There have been moments where I considered making that call and at the last moment, I manage to create a genuine sexual experience.

If you read my column, you know that I hold my male readers to a high standard. Once you cross that line of putting out money and making a woman have sex with you, you lose the status of gentleman, at least for the time being. You can get it back over time, but your batting average takes a hit. If this is not the first time that you've hired a pro, then by all means, bargain hard and don't bother paying extra for oral because it won't be worth it if you are already paying for the main event.

Just know that while you might be making your night a success, you are also contributing to an industry that enslaves women and forces mothers and daughters to sacrifice control of their body just so you can get your dick wet. For god 's sake, wear a condom. Take it to your grave afterwards because no one wants to know that you are slimy enough to pay for sex, especially your girlfriend or future wife. Best of luck, remember that you matter most!

Mr. Slumpty Dumpty

"I have had a few short relationships lately, and the last girl I asked out said she was too busy. What's with this run of bad luck? Usually when I meet someone and I'm interested in them, it works out pretty well. What am I doing wrong?"

You see your situation as bad luck, but you are actually doing everything right. You are putting yourself out in the world and meeting girls, you are asking them out and going on dates, and you are able to see the reasons why the ones that get away go away. To see where you are at in a different light, think about your clone that is doing the opposite of what you are doing.

He is staying at home, afraid to go out because he doesn't want to risk being rejected. He is watching too much porn, masturbating to climax fast, and training himself to be a premature ejaculator. Your clone is the one that hangs out with friends and says, "I would do her," but never makes a move.

While you are not seeing the fruits of your labor, you are making yourself available for the right girl. Even the best hitters go into slumps. One girl might be crazy, another might use you for a rebound, but you can learn from every interaction. Each new person you interact with gives you an opportunity for batting practice. The last rejection is the first step towards the next acceptance. Take rejection as a compliment and you can change your entire outlook on dating. Instead of loser logic, "yes means yes and no means ruphies" you can practice "yes means yes, and no means not with me".

Take anything but a yes as a strike out, and move on with your pride intact. The girl that rejects you is doing every other girl on earth a favor. The worst thing you can do is take yourself out of the game. Instead of retiring, take your game to the minor leagues and make dates to practice different things. Have a lunch date to practice your listening, a dinner to practice chivalry. Eventually you will be an all star again.

I suppose the real lesson here is to not masturbate for less than 15 minutes at a time, and try not to let a string of rejections get you down. Think of them as short red lights on a long commute. Best of luck, remember that you matter most!

Mr. Ready to Order

"I am attracted to a girl that works at the restaurant that I frequent with my buddies. I want to ask her out, but I am shy, and when my friends and I go there we tend to get loud and obnoxious. I am afraid that she will reject me because of that, and also if things don't go well for the two of us, we will have to see each other every time I come to the restaurant. Do you think I should go for it?"

I know how hard finding a place where the drink specials are decent can be in a big city. Coming from a college town I have been spoiled. I have been a part of the group mentality when guys just want to have fun. Drinks are knocked over, curse words fly over to surrounding booths, and every woman in the building becomes some part of an "I bet you won't" challenge.

Being attracted to women servers is a biological instinct that creates feeling of being provided for and attentiveness to a man. We associate her work with our pleasure. After all, they say the way to a mans heart is through his stomach. It doesn't hurt when the waitress is sexy and has a skimpy outfit on, either. You have two dilemmas to overcome if you want to woo the waitress. The first is the establishment, and the second is your association.

This waitress gets hit on all the time for all the reasons I just mentioned. What you need to do is take the rules of engagement and bend them like Beckham. Instead of approaching her while all of your friends are there to support you and cheer you on and to make a scene, you are going to make your way to the place when there are few people there, early on in her shift before she is stressed and tired from standing and serving Neanderthals such as you and your friends, eating and drinking like they are back at the cave.

Assuming you know her name, and you do, because you can see it on her name tag (or ask someone) you will get her one on one in her comfort zone. You will have to grow a pair for this one, so maybe have a drink at the bar first. Engage her by name; "Hi (insert name here) I'm (insert your name here). I come here often with my very loud friends for (trivia night/happy hour/whatever you do there). I don't make a habit of asking out strangers, I'm actually a pretty shy guy most of the time. But, I admire the way that you always (insert your favorite detailed observation about her personality), and I think you might be someone worth getting to know outside of (name of restaurant).

Join me for XXX on Xday?"

That's all there is to it. It's short enough to memorize and gentle enough not to come off like a stalker. If it doesn't work then it's nothing that you did. She doesn't like the way you look or your table manners. It really doesn't matter which. Here is why it will work. The intro is simple enough; you establish who you are and why you know her. It will help jog her memory as well, so I hope you made a good impression. By saying that you don't ask out every girl you meet, you show that you are selective and that is a hidden compliment to her. When you admit to your shyness, it shows that you are not afraid to share insecurity, and will build rapport that should help transform her from stoic waitress to a care bear.

The detail statement is crucial because it will show that you are observant of her actions and that you desire her. Do not stare at her tits as you say the line. The detail could be that she wears the same earrings each time or that she is always smiling, or she has cute frames some days, and contacts on others. Say nothing about onion booty, DSL's, or any other physical trait you would pick out with your friends. Make it something that you wouldn't see if she walked past you just once.

You tell her that she has peaked your interest and that you want to get to know her as a person, not just the girl bringing buckets of beer. That shows that you are not using her for her employee discount (not yet). After your monologue calmly ask for her phone number. When she gives it, tell her, "Thanks, have a great shift." Call her the next afternoon to ask how her work was, and set up a date (I suggest pedicures for her sore footsies), You two can learn about each other while she associates you with positive physical feelings (unless her feet are jacked up). Best of luck, remember that you matter most!

Mr. Go Out With a Bang

"I found out that my position at work is being eliminated in six months. I have been good about not sleeping around until now, but when I got this news, I imagined myself making up for lost time with at least a couple of coworkers before I am out the door. Is there any reason why I shouldn't let loose? It seems like at least one girl would be up for it. "

Given the current economic climate, you are not the only one that might be in this position. Normally I am against any kind of work relationship due to the gossip that usually surrounds these kinds of hook-ups, but in your case, I say let the good times roll. The best way to get over bad news is to make some good things happen. If you feel safe enough in your current role that a relationship with a stable minded woman coworker won't push you out the door faster, then go for it. Be sure that this woman is not the jealous type when the relationship comes to an end, otherwise you might have to add sexual harasser to your freshly minted resume.

If you let her know ahead of time that you are out no matter what, then she has the decision to make, not you. If she is for the cubicle couple thing it can be a socially productive six months. If you want to go Don Juan and try to lay as many coworkers as possible, you better tread lightly. You want to make sure you get the letters of recommendation in hand before you do anything to ruin your chance at the next job. Go ahead and try to sleep with someone higher on the food chain, maybe they will put in a good word for you. Best of luck, remember that you matter most!

Ms. Cubicle Crush

"I have a crush on my coworker. We work together on almost a daily basis, and we often hang out in the same group after work. I know that dating at work is supposed to be a no-no but I think he likes me, and my coworkers think so too. What do you think I should do about it?"

It is natural to have feelings for those that you work with on a daily basis. Being in close quarters, sharing tasks, and spending eight hours a day together brings people together longer, and often closer than our out-of-work relationships. Add to that a physical attraction, and the workplace suddenly transforms into Temptation Island. I have been there and done that when I was a young buck. I never had a problem with the crossover. There are some questions that you need to address before you dive into the copy room with your business beau.

How are you doing at work right now? Are you getting high marks on your performance reviews? People at work would love to see you hook up with your crush, because there is nothing that office mates like more than some drama to go along with their spreadsheets and emails. If you are not on your game with your work, people will blame it on your relationship, and that can affect your well-being.

A good friend once told me not to shit where you eat; meaning not to mess up your ability to earn a living. If you are ready to be the whisper of the office for better or worse, then go for it. How will you handle it if it doesn't work out for the better? Try going through your workday pretending that he broke your heart or that the sex was a disaster, and see how you function with the two of you being in the same place working on shared tasks. Does the idea of being in the same cafeteria with a man that you queefed on turn you off?

If you are both mature enough to keep your work separate from your dirty work, then maybe it can work. If this is a part time job that you don't care about, then by all means bring your work home with you tonight. Make sure that you think about the pros and cons before you act on that crush. If this man is your boss, you need to think twice. Best of luck, remember that you matter most!

SEX
Ms. Turn Two

"I have been building a friendship with two guys at the same time, both of them are friends and they work at the same place. I have not done anything to make it seem I like one more than the other, but I think that it is time that I have to make a choice. I would really love to try and sleep with both of them, and they seem like the kind of guys that just might do it. I have no clue how to even bring it up, what can I do?"

I admire your ambition to try and bed both of these guys, but I am going to bring you back to earth for a minute. These guys are close, so that means they talk, and no doubt they have talked about you. You have to assume the sex conversation has come up already. You may or may not have a chance to sleep with either one of them, but I will tell you the best way to make the double play.

Because these men are friends and they work together, timing might be a problem. What I would recommend is that instead of trying to bed each one separately, you go for the gold and try for the threesome. Women friends are sometimes just one too many drinks away from a make out session, but guys let loose a bit differently. If you can get them feeling comfortable, you could get these two to make a man sandwich out of you. While chatting away, ask if they have ever messed around, then suggest with confidence that you all go home and go to bed together. "It will be fun."

Your other option is the back to back, which might make for better chances of success, but will probably end both relationships. Men might seem open, but jealousy and a respect for the friendship might prevent either one from sleeping with you. After all, bros before hoes is a guy commandment, for better or worse. Ask one guy to hang out during a time that the other is working, then use the killer instinct to seal the deal. The same day, before the dudes can communicate too much, be ready to enjoy the company of the one just getting off of work, ideally when the other man is going in for his shift.

Netflix and chill a double feature by pumping up the ego of guy number two, and don't mention what happened earlier other than to say that you had a good time hanging out with the other man. Be prepared for the backlash from both guys, but you do you girl. There is no reason for hard feelings, sometimes friends have sex. For Gods sake, use a condom each time. Maybe you will get lucky twice and end up being in a sitcom plot with two new sex partners. Best of luck, remember that you matter most!

Mr. What's in a Number?

"During my last date, the girl asked about how many partners I have had. I dodged the question, but I am afraid it is going to come up gain. From what I have heard from her, I think that my number is going to be way higher than hers, is there a way to avoid this all together?"

It's funny that our priorities change as we get older. When we are young men we are taught that more is better. We try and get our numbers up as high as possible to brag to our friends and feel like a stud. When we get out of college, we are left with knowledge of our conquests, but often we have no one that shares in the more is merrier prerogative.

If you are lucky enough to get out of the lothario lifestyle without an STD, then you have great strength in the battle to keep your promiscuous past where it belongs. The next time she asks about the number of women you have put yourself inside, tell her that a gentleman does not kiss and tell, but you want her to know that you are safe and disease free. If you aren't, then this is the time to tell her. Make sure that she doesn't tell you her number, then you will be on the hook to disclose as well.

Tell her that you appreciate why she wants to know, but that it doesn't matter to you to know hers or to tell her yours. Don't ask, don't tell. Save the sex stories for the homecoming weekends at the frat house. Never give out details about your sexual past to new relationships until you are well committed. Act like it is the first time every time. Treat her like a mystery, and you will be rewarded. Best of luck, remember that you matter most!

Ms. Size Queen

"Is there any way to tell the size of a guy's cock by the other parts of his body? Is the stereotype of big hands or feet true? What about the race of the guy? My girlfriends all have different opinions. What's the real deal?"

During our youth we learn that our naked bodies are not to be seen by others. Our parents teach us that for our own safety, just like "Don't talk to strangers," and "Stop-look-listen before crossing the street". Young men learn to change quickly in group settings such as locker rooms so that they don't have to be around other naked dudes, because it is a bad thing. We have to use urinals that don't always have dividers or any privacy to them. We are taught to keep our eyes straight forward and not to talk.

A boy lives in isolation with his penis for most of his young life and into adulthood. Boys that see their father naked are not any more educated because they have a skewed perspective of penis size, since they are looking up at their father, and some boys don't have any adult male in their life. For some guys, the first experience of seeing other penises comes when they begin to see pornography. As a boy matures, so does his penis.

Much like women, some are early starters and some are late bloomers. Men that grow up in penile isolation begin to wonder how they stack up compared to others, but they have no outlet to reassure them that they are normal, or to even know what normal means. A boy sees his penis as a teenager compared to Long Dong Silver and other porn stars, and that begins the feelings of inadequacy that sometimes last into adulthood. Adult men don't talk about it together; most penis publicity comes from the females.

What are the ladies saying about penis size? In the porn they are shouting about how big a cock is, women get together and out comes a "he was small" or "he was huge" but even these women don't know what average means. Knowledge is power for both sexes. The penis you see as a woman is not the penis that the man sees when he looks down. Only one thing can be agreed on by both sexes, that a penis and balls are very silly looking.

A man looks directly down onto his penis which gives it an appearance of being smaller than it actually is. The penis as an organ connects to the body far within the pelvis and therefore is much more than what you see on the outside; just like the clitoris. What you see on the outside can vary based on blood flow, temperature, and arousal. An erection can vary by a quarter of an inch less or more based on those things. Some men are growers and some men are showers. The average size of men across the world is between five and six inches.

Penis size is as varied as breast size or foot size or finger length or nail bed depth. Don't hold any stereotype to be true, and you will learn to appreciate the penis in front of you as unique and full of potential. Your vagina can stretch wide enough to give birth and during arousal it lengthens to twice the resting size. The vagina also molds itself to the shape of the same penis over time. You become a custom fit for that penis. The vagina walls are full of nerve endings from the vulva up a few inches on the inside. The deeper you get, the less pleasure sensing nerves you have up there. Physically, any man with a few inches should be enough to feed the needy.

The size issue for men is comparable to the weight issue for women. One of the greatest things a man can do for himself is to become comfortable with his penis. The modern man is full of insecurities, and a little knowledge can go a long way. Now that you have some information, you can make an informed decision on the next guy you lay eyes on. If you see a man you like with small hands and small feet it doesn't mean that he won't have a great big, massive, throbbing heart. Best of luck, remember that you matter most!

Mr. Careful What You Wish For

"The new girl I am dating is a lot of fun. We get along well, and she is very sexual. She sends me naughty text messages during the day, and she has all sorts of kinky ideas. I thought I was open to that kind of thing, but I am a bit worried that I am too boring for her, or that she is really some kind of crazy sex freak that is going to give me a disease. What can I do to keep up, and how do I bring up the STD thing?"

Back in my day, I always felt a sense of enjoyment when I found a girl that was comfortable enough to explore with me sexually. There are few things more fun than learning about another person while enjoying sensuous pleasures at the same time. The kind of sex that keeps you up all night, and sends you off to work the next day not concerned about the lack of sleep, that's the good stuff. Now that I am just a tad bit removed from the debauchery days of our lives, I have a slightly different perspective on super freaks. Let me preface this advice by saying it takes two to tango, so you are also a dirty boy fornicator.

The first thing you need to do is find out if this girl's crotch or throat is on fire before you put your man clit anywhere near them without some kind of shield. It may be too late if you have already been testing the waters, but before you dive in head first, you need to ask her some questions, and give some answers of your own. It doesn't matter how many partners she has had, it just matters if she is safe.

She may count differently than you. She might have slept with the basketball team, but only counted the guy that went to the NBA. Ask her if she has a condom before the next time you guys know you are going to have sex. If not, you can ask her how she feels about contraceptives and birth control. You guys can go the store and pick out her favorite condom. No one likes condoms but most people like condoms more than babies or genital warts, so keep that in mind. I like to throw out the question, "Have you ever been tested before," because that usually flows into when and what were the results.

If you have not been tested in the last six months, go do it! A clean report card is a great aphrodisiac. You can even have a date to get tested, and use the excuse that you like her, and want to make sure you are both safe because you haven't been tested in a while. Ask her if she has ever had cold sores, because cold sores are herpes too. That will help you feel safer being with a freak, but now you need to arm yourself with tools and techniques to keep up with the girl.

Any bookstore (maybe not Christian bookstores) will have an aisle dedicated to sexuality and self help stuff. Venture down there and pick up a few books with titles like "100 ways to do it" and "Be the biggest freak you can". That will be a fun date too, and will give you a starting point to build on. Let her be the freak, you do the details on the dates, and you will make quite a dynamic duo. Praise her and all those like her for being open. Wrap it up and enjoy yourself! Best of luck, remember that you matter most!

Ms. Unequal Opportunity

"I only have sex with black men, and my friends say that I am wrong to limit myself to that race. I am a full figured white woman, and I think my friends are being racist. Which of us are right?"

You and your friends are both wrong, but for different reasons. You only have sex with black men, but why didn't you say you only date black men? From what you present, it sounds like you are being just as racist as they are. Since you and your friends are stereotyping, allow me to do the same. There is a possibility that you are only attracted to black men, the way some men are only attracted to blonds, and that's ok, preference is preference. We can't force ourselves to be attracted to someone that we're not. But, if that is not the case, consider that maybe you only sleep with black men because you believe that society has pushed you into a corner. You are stereotyping white, brown, yellow, and men of all other skin tones as not being receptive to you. You see what you call "black" men as a safe place to be free sexually because there is a stereotype in American society that black men appreciate a woman with meat on their bones.

You seek out the people that make you feel

good about yourself, and comfortable with your body. That is great for the people that are having sex with you, but why are you just having sex with them and not pursuing a relationship? Maybe you are holding back because of your own prejudice, or maybe you only desire sex right now. Both options are probably valid. Where your logic breaks down is after you have sex with any person, they lose interest unless there is something to keep our attention. A man (unless they are a dog) wants to be with a woman that values herself and believes they are beautiful, which is how the stereotype about confident black women got started.

If you truly felt good about yourself and thought you were beautiful, you wouldn't need others to make you feel good; you would already feel good about yourself. You wouldn't limit yourself to any ethnicity, only to men that value the kind of person you are. Your friends only want you to be happy, and they might be racist, but that isn't where their concern stems from (I hope). They want you to be with one person (or people) that makes you happy. There is nothing wrong with sexual freedom as long as you are being safe about it , if that is your goal. You shouldn't limit yourself to any culture. Turn men into your own personal buffet if you like, but do not stereotype one person from any culture as representing the entire group. That's how the "All men are dogs" stereotype got started. Although I consider myself to ethnically unbiased, I bet if you look back at my Tinder swipes, you would find more dark featured women and not too many blondes or African American women. I lived in Asia the entire time I have used the apps, so I can't say that my options have been too diverse. Whenever I returned to America for a break, I am drawn to the thick thighs, butts, and breasts that tend to be missing in Asia.

I have been lucky to see and experience individuals from everywhere, and I would hate the idea that I was limited to only one look or ethnicity. Try opening up your preferences and you might find that you can be appreciated by a range of gentlemen, and you don't have to give up the sex you are having now while you do. Best of luck, remember that you matter most!

Ms. Lonely and Lustful

"Every now and then I take a guy home for the night to have sex. It is usually fun in the moment, but afterwards I feel trashy and then I get kind of depressed and lonely. I don't ever want to run into the guy again. I have friends that enjoy their one-night stands and they don't seem to have the sad feelings afterwards. How can I stop feeling bad about wanting to get laid?"

I understand the desire to have hot sex with a stranger every blue moon (or every night). Everyone has desire and we have all succumbed to a moment of passion at some point in our lives. The outcome for these romantic trysts is going to be different depending on what you are bringing into the bedroom. By that, I don't mean handcuffs or whipped cream. The feelings that spur you to action might not be as shallow as a desire to hump the hot guy in the bar. I have seen firsthand how a hook up can turn into a letdown because of the motivation behind the deed.

I know a young woman that seemed to have everything going right for her in life. She was in a great city with plenty of options for romantic partnerships. She couldn't find a gentleman that was interested in her as a person; they only wanted to use her to cum, but not to date exclusively. She would entertain her desires when she felt the itch. She liked the positive attention from a man, but she had the same negative emotions afterwards when they revealed their true intentions or lack there of.

Her behavior may be seen as promiscuous to some, but her motivation comes not from sexual desire, it comes from loneliness and emotional insecurity with herself. Some people that are lonely get a pet to satisfy their desire to be loved and feel appreciated.

This girl would search for acceptance and appreciation from strange gentleman. When she is left alone with just her thoughts, she knows that she is just as lonely as she was before she went out to the bar to get laid, and that she had put herself at risk for more than just a hangover. She may have felt fulfilled during sex, but no penis is long enough to fill the space in a lonely heart.

When I was on the Tyra Banks show to discuss the behavior of promiscuous girls, I met young women that treat themselves like a hotel room. They allow men to check in, mess up the sheets, and check out. They had deep emotional needs to feel loved that they were not meeting. If that is how you feel, then it is best to put the dicks down for a minute and work on the reason you are picking them up in the first place.

You are worthy of being treated with respect and you should hold yourself to high standards. If you are lonely, you should remedy that with your heart and your mind, because you can't do it with your vagina. When you go out, try not to mask your emotions with alcohol and decide ahead of time what you are willing to do. Once the excuses are gone, you can focus on finding a man that will embrace you for the content of your character, not just the access to your body's soft spots.

Learn to value yourself as an individual and you can flip lonely into independent. Then you can enjoy your fits of friskiness and embrace your sexuality for the right reasons, and you will become the envy of your friends. Hookups are fantastic when we are coming from a place of self-love and confidence. It's hard to remain sex positive if you are feeling negative about yourself. Best of luck, remember that you matter most!

Ms. Cockoholic

"I am a healthy woman that takes a partner every so often, but lately I have been super horny. What is making me so over-the-top randy? I don't have a steady partner, but the urge is getting the best of me. Taking matters into my own hands isn't helping."

Wanting sex is sign that your body is functioning normally. Being that you are a woman, the stereotype is that you do not compartmentalize your feelings, so everything in your life is probably going well. Disclaimer: If you have a history of manic behaviors, you might want to check in with your counselor if you notice other related symptoms.

What you need to do is prepare yourself for a safe release of that sexual tension. Most women do this using what they call Tinder or a boyfriend, but the reality is that these girls could be using a man for his penis and occasional meals, and they don't want to feel guilty about that. I suggest you look in the little black book and circle the name of the man that you feel most comfortable with.

You don't want to be self-conscious around your sex toy. Make sure that you do not use a penis that is attached to somebody you have an emotional attachment with, because that will complicate the primal urges to feel pleasure with feelings of "Where is this going". Explain the conditions of your intended relationship over a drink, and then stick to your rules.

Let him know that your crotch is on fire and you want to use his fire hose to put it out, as often as you feel the need. You will get no complaint from him. Use protection (before he tests the waters) because the fastest way to kill a dick buzz is with an accidental pregnancy. If an accident happens, don't forget that Plan-B is a trip to the pharmacy or Planned Parenthood away (hundreds of miles away for some now) and works for up to three days after sex. Best of luck, remember that you matter most!

Ms. Miracle Worker

"My current lover is not as good a lover as my last relationship. I know that guys don't want to hear that they are bad in bed, but I want him to know how I like to do it. What do I say to get what I want without hurting his feelings?"

Working with an inept lover is a lot like teaching the blind. Explaining things using words alone will not do much good. You are going to have to take matters into your own hands. To begin the conversation, I suggest you take this lump of a lover out for drinks. After the both of you are tipsy, ask him what he likes in bed. Let him tell you. He may or may not be bright enough to ask you what you like, so you need to take the initiative and let him know.

Share the feelings you like to have, be carefree with your language, and make it hot. When you are done with your vodka/tonics and beers, go home and practice what you preach. Tell him to please you, and after he does, you will please him, but not before. Make him learn the places you like rubbed, the pressure you desire from his touch. When he begins to show some competency, you make sure that he does not forget...by rewarding him for his efforts. Each time you begin to play, reinforce when he does the right thing, and he will soon be the lover you want him to be, even if he isn't always the person you want to be with. Best of luck, remember that you matter most!

Mr. Tough Love

"The girl I started seeing recently told me that she likes to get rough during sex. I don't feel comfortable manhandling this girl, I am a lot bigger than her and I'm afraid I might hurt her, for one, and I think it is a bit too close to rape. Is it a lost cause dating this girl; or do you think we I should try to compromise some?"

Most guys were raised to be respectful to women at all times. Most women were raised to be polite and dainty. When dainty and respectful have sex, it seems very puritan. Of course, sex brings out the primal instincts in both men and women, so things can get a bit rough at times. Many women have a fantasy of being dominated in some way; just look at any random romance novel.

In the real world, girls that have been abused sometimes grow up to have patterns of wanting to be roughed up during sex. There are all kinds of ways that you as the man can interpret your lady friend's desire to get slapped around or choked, some people are just kinky for the love of kink. I suggest you leave the psychoanalysis to the experts and take this woman as she is, a glutton for punishment. Make sure you find out exactly what she likes, and what her comfort levels are. If you like this girl, it may seem hard to slap her in the face during sex because you wouldn't do it outside the bedroom. You might feel good about spanking her ass a bit, but there is a fine line between pulling her hair back and pulling her hair out.

Sure, you might feel like a dirt bag afterwards, but let this girl take you out of your comfort zone for a change. Her kink isn't your problem, because you are not going to make it your problem. I am a pacifist in real life and in the bedroom, but if a girl I was comfortable with asked me to hit her over the head with a lamp as she was getting hers, I might do it once, after she signed a waiver. Depending on how I felt afterwards, I might have to pull the plug. You will have a great sexy girl story for life, and you can let this girl know that it isn't in your nature to be that rough, so you want to stay friends only.

She will understand because you have already established that you are that kind of person. If you really like this girl and see her level of pain seeking as beyond safe, ask her to go to counseling, because you are enabling her psychosis if you continue. It doesn't make you any less of a man to prefer not to hurt someone. If you are willing to push your own boundaries, make sure you have a first aid kit in the nightstand and a safety word on the tip of your tongue. Best of luck, remember that you matter most!

Mr. Employee of the Month

"I started a new job recently and I ended up sleeping with my coworker after the first week. I don't want a relationship with her, but she seems to be interested in more than casual sex. How do I cool her down and not make things awkward?"

We can't go back to that night and take your penis out of her vagina, but we can do some damage control so that the two of you can work together long enough for you to get fired for something non-sex related. Having sex with a coworker is rarely worth the fall out. No matter how hot your office hook up looks, you need to make it crystal clear that that is not your typical behavior and you will not let it happen again.

Whether it is true or not, you have to let her know that you care about yours and her office reputations, and you know people love to spread rumors. Even though you really enjoyed yourself with her, it means a lot to you to keep the job and keep her as a friend. You cannot (will not) do that if you keep having sex. In order for that to fly you can't pork any other coworkers for at least a few months. By then she will have gotten over the idea of you and her, and she will move on to someone she thinks will make you jealous. Only then is it safe to hump your cubicle neighbor and start the game all over again. Sometimes, we just can't help ourselves. Best of luck, remember that you matter most!

SEASON ONE SUMMARY

The interactions we have as we develop friendships, have our sexual needs met, and bring people into our worlds have a tremendous effect on how we feel from one day to the next. Each of the preceding questions came from people seeking answers to clarify and confirm their beliefs. From high school students to middle aged men and women, the brave people that sought advice from me are starting to practice the EGA in their lives.

We are accountable for our actions, we seek to meet our needs without harming others as much as possible. We do not judge others for how they live their lives, and we strive to be the best version of ourselves we can. Embracing the EGA can help you move from the initial attraction and baby steps towards courtships as we build a shared history with potential partners.

You Matter Most! Season Two will show you the questions and answers that arise as we enter, maintain, and leave more committed relationships. *Season Three* will cover marriages, family, and friendships.

Please head over to Amazon to review the book as you finish. Every purchase and review helps my visibility to other readers that might benefit from the EGA as well. I am eternally grateful to you for taking the time to read my work. I feel a calling to help others, and I hope my insights have given you something to think about, as well as a bit of entertainment. Thank you, and remember, YOU MATTER MOST!

ABOUT THE AUTHOR

Ethan Gregory began in the helping profession in the mid-1990s. His education in psychology, sexual health, dating, and parenting gives him a wide base of knowledge to help others. Providing social services, therapy, and school guidance honed his skills in mental health. He earned his doctoral degree in Counseling Psychology in 2014 from Argosy University, studying dating preferences. He has lived in America, China and Japan working as a counselor. He empowers his readers on an array of subject matters.

Follow him on Twitter, @drethangregory.

Facebook at facebook.com/drethangregory.

His homepage is www.drethangregory.com. You can sign up for his reader list there to get advance copies of his next books as well as hear about his sex-help adventures.

www.ingramcontent.com/pod-product-compliance
Lightning Source LLC
Chambersburg PA
CBHW021201020426
42331CB00003B/160